WATERFORD

THROUGH TIME

Colm Long

AMBERLEY PUBLISHING

View on the Quay, Waterford

Waterford Quay, *c.* 1900
Waterford's Quay, once known as 'the noblest quay in Europe', is a mile long, from Grattan Quay to Adelphi Quay. It has been said in times gone by that it was possible to travel its entire length by never setting foot on land, such was the density of ships tied up at the quayside.

First published 2014

Amberley Publishing
The Hill, Stroud, Gloucestershire, GL5 4EP
www.amberley-books.com

Copyright © Colm Long, 2014

The right of Colm Long to be identified as the Author
of this work has been asserted in accordance with the
Copyrights, Designs and Patents Act 1988.

ISBN 978 1 4456 3941 3 (print)
ISBN 978 1 4456 3953 6 (ebook)

British Library Cataloguing in Publication Data.
A catalogue record for this book is available from the
British Library.

Typesetting by Amberley Publishing.
Printed in Great Britain.

Introduction

The name Waterford is derived from the old Norse word *Vedrarfjiordr*, meaning 'ram fjord' or 'windy fjord'. The Irish name *Port Láirge* can be translated as 'leg shaped port'. The old Celtic name for Waterford was *Cuan na Gréine,* or 'The Harbour of the Sun'.

Founded in 914, Waterford is Ireland's oldest city. Captured by Strongbow in 1170, it was here that Henry II landed in 1171. He was the first King of England to set foot in Ireland. Throughout the following 800 years, Waterford remained close to the English monarchy. The city's motto, *Urbs Intacta Manet Waterfordia,* or 'Waterford Remains The Untaken City', was given by Henry VII following an unsuccessful attack on the city by Perkin Warbeck, a pretender to the throne. In the sixteenth century, Waterford was considered to be a city state, when William Wyse became its own direct emissary to the court of Henry VIII.

In the seventeenth century, Waterford was the only Irish city to hold out against Cromwell, although it surrendered to his son-in-law, Gen. Ireton, later. The eighteenth century saw Waterford transformed. New public buildings were erected under the watchful eye of Waterford architect John Roberts; these included both cathedrals and the city hall. Waterford Crystal gained international reputation in the nineteenth century. A shipbuilding industry also developed and was second only to Belfast in terms of tonnage produced.

In the early years of the twentieth century, when many of the images here were taken, Waterford was described in a newspaper report as having 'wealth and poverty, gaiety and rags, music and weeping, sobriety and drunkenness, religion and immorality'.

Today, Waterford has a unique blend of the old and modern. The ancient city walls and towers are interspersed with modern shopping centres. The rejuvenation of the Viking Triangle has brought history alive and it has become the cultural centre of the city. In the county, the town of Dungarvan forms the commercial heart. The other towns and villages have retained their charm and character into the modern age.

Acknowledgements

Those interested in Waterford history in the early twentieth century are lucky; one of the most prolific photographers in the country, A. H. Poole, was from Waterford and operated from his studio here. While its business was mainly portraiture, the firm also published a vast array of postcards of local scenes. Poole's collection of over 65,000 glass negatives are now stored in the National Library. This made the job of collecting old postcards very easy.

However, to do justice to the breadth and depth of both city and county, I needed more than postcards. The National Library proved an invaluable resource, and I have included fourteen images from their achives in the book. Waterford County Museum has done fantastic work in collecting old photographs from the county, and these are readily accessible on their website. They were very generous in allowing me to include a number of their images. Jane Rothwell in the Waterford City Archives allowed me access to the Annie Brophy collection, and I have used a number of her images also. The Local Studies Room in Waterford City Library also has a collection of old Waterford postcards, of which several have been included in the book.

Paul O'Farrell kindly allowed me to use two of his postcards. Oliver Lupton and Pat Hennessy each provided me with one of their own photographs. Eamonn McEneaney of Waterford Museum of Treasures gave me permission to use the image of the Van der Hagen oil painting of Waterford from 1736. James Eogan from the National Roads Authority gave me permission to use the reconstruction of the image from the Great Charter Roll, which was published in their book, *Cois tSiúire*.

All but two of the modern photographs were taken by myself. Thanks to the Tower Hotel for allowing me access to the roof of the hotel in order to take the shot of Reginald's Tower. The aerial shot of the Viking Triangle was taken by Mick Malone of Déise Aerial Photoraphy, and the shot of the Tower Hotel in 2010 was taken by Declan McGrath.

A number of friends helped out in identifying dates for old postcards. Thanks to Oliver Lupton, Pat Hennessy, Tony Barden and Tim Sherman. Special thanks to Tim for his knowledge of old cars, which narrowed down the years.

A special thanks goes to Declan McGrath for his encouragement and guidance throughout, especially his photographic help.

Finally, this book would not have happened without the encouragement and support of my wife, Jenifer, and my children, Deirdre, Brendan and Stephen.

Waterford City, 1373
This illustration from the Great Charter Roll, held in the Waterford Museum of Treasures, is the earliest surviving image of any Irish city. The medieval city is displayed with brightly coloured roofs and white walls. Reginald's Tower and a number of churches are also shown. The rabbit warren in the foreground, and the salmon leaping in the Suir, introduce an interesting pastoral element to the image.

Waterford City, 1736 and *c.* 1895

The earliest painting of an Irish city is the oil painting of Waterford by Van Der Hagen, 1736. It cost the Corporation of the time £20, with the frame costing another £4. The painting is still on display in the Bishop's Palace Museum in Waterford. It would be another fifty-eight years before the first bridge was built across the Suir in 1794. This bridge, nicknamed 'Timbertoes', was a toll bridge that served the city of Waterford for the next century.

The Bridge & General View, Waterford. 1475.

Redmond Bridge, *c.* 1940

Waterford Corporation purchased Timbertoes in 1907, and it was made toll free on 31 December 1907. Within a few years, the wooden bridge was demolished and replaced by a steel structure. John Redmond, MP and leader of the Irish Parliamentary Party, opened the new Redmond Bridge in February 1913. This bridge only lasted seventy-three years, and was replaced by Rice Bridge in 1986.

City from Cromwell's Rock, *c.* 1895
This panoramic view of the Suir shows the long quayside lined with ships. The Adelphi Hotel is the large building in the middle of the picture, with a steamship docked in front on Adelphi Quay. The spire of Christ Church Cathedral dominates the skyline. In the distance, a sailing ship can be seen going through the central opening arch of Timbertoes.

Train Station, c. 1900

The train station was built in 1864. It was known as Waterford North. Waterford South station was on the other side of the river in Bilberry. On the right of the picture are two public houses that were demolished in 1903 to make way for line improvements to New Ross and Rosslare. The building was demolished in 1967 and replaced by the present structure, which opened in 1969. It was renamed Plunkett station after Joseph Plunkett, one of the executed leaders of the 1916 Rising.

Reginald's Tower, *c.* 1895 and 1945

Reginald's Tower is no doubt the most recognisable landmark in Waterford. Built on the site of an original Viking fort, it dates from approximately 1185 and is Ireland's oldest civic building. It has had many uses through the centuries, including a mint and a prison. The tower was the residence of the High Constable at the time of both of these scenes, and remained so until 1954. The tower is now part of Waterford Museum of Treasures and hosts an exhibition of Viking Waterford.

Reginald's Tower, c. 1960
The square tower in the right of the picture is an ESB transformer tower. This was one of four in the city. The others were located at the Clock Tower, the Bridge and Ballybricken. Built in 1929, they were demolished in 1972. The transit sheds on the quayside have been replaced by the William Vincent Wallace Millennium Plaza. In the far distance, Fleming's castle can be seen on the hill. This was demolished in 1969 to make way for the construction of the Ardree Hotel.

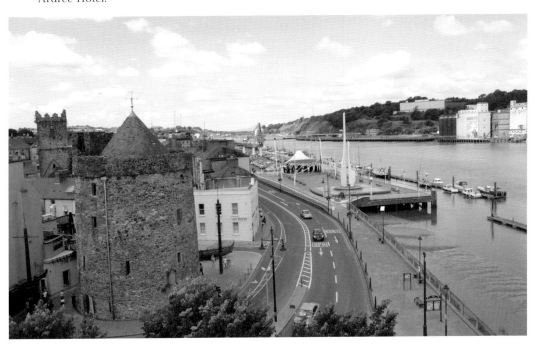

Reginald's Tower.

Poole Photographers, *c.* 1900

The building to the right of Reginald's Tower is Poole's Stores. The family firm of A. H. Poole operated as commercial photographers in Waterford between the years 1884 and 1954. During this time, they took an extremely large number of photographs, and some 65,000 glass negatives are now in the National Library in Dublin. In addition to the shop on the Quay, they also had a studio on The Mall. A replica Viking ship now occupies this space.

Parade Quay, c. 1895
This is a busy quayside with a mixture of sailing and steam ships berthed. The post office, built in 1876, stands out as the landmark building. The sign for Kirwan's Provision Store is the present location of La Fontana restaurant, beside Jordan's bar. Interesting points to note are the top hat on the gentleman driving the horse-drawn carriage and also the uniform of the sailor in the bottom left-hand corner.

View on the Quay, Waterford

Clock Tower, *c.* 1900 and *c.* 1950

The Clock Tower is another well known landmark in Waterford. It was built in 1864 for the regulation of shipping and cost £200, while the clock mechanism cost an extra £78 10s. The building at the corner of the Quay and Barronstrand Street, in the photograph below, is the Provincial Bank of Ireland, later the AIB Bank, which was built in 1908. The premises beside it was O'Brien's Model Bakeries and Café. This was later demolished and the bank extended.

THE QUAYS, WATERFORD

Clock Tower, c. 1965

Unfortunately, the ESB when choosing to position transformers, decided to build transformer towers at the most inappropriate places, such as directly beside the Clock Tower. A similar tower was built directly opposite Reginald's Tower and can be seen on page 11. Some of the vehicles seen here include a Commer Van, Hilman Minx, an Austin A40 and a CIE horse delivery cart. Perhaps the yellow box was an early attempt at containerisation.

Meagher's Quay, 1900

The Bank of Ireland building was built *c.* 1875, and it retains all of its original features today. However, the adjoining buildings were all demolished in the 1960s and replaced by Shaws Department Store. These included P. Tobin and Sons, drapers, G. Walpole, grocer, and N. Harvey & Co., printers and stationers. The last building on the block was the premises of Robertson, Ledlie, Ferguson and Co. This building remains today.

The Fair, Ballybricken, Waterford.

Photo by A. H. Poole, Waterford.

Ballybricken Fair, *c.* 1900

Fairs have been held in Waterford since King John first granted a charter in 1204. In recent centuries they were held on the hill of Ballybricken, normally on the first Monday of every month. The fair eventually ceased in 1955 with the introduction of marts. The house on the corner, now occupied by Ned Kelly's Pub, was an old style grocery store and public house, advertised as 'M. Walsh Tea, Wine, Whiskey and Provision Stores'.

The Mall, *c.* 1939

Old maps of Waterford show that the present-day Mall was actually covered in water and known as Miller's Marsh. This was filled in 1737 and laid out as a tree-lined promenade, and replaced with paving stone in 1792. Very little has changed on the left-hand side of the street from 1939 (*seen here*). At the end of the street, the Tower Hotel has replaced the Adelphi and Imperial Hotels. Behind the trees on the right-hand side was the Bishop Foy School, demolished in 1967 to make way for ESB offices, now Waterford Crystal Showroom.

Broad Street, c. 1890

This is a wide, open space occupied by just one horse and cart. Most of the buildings on the right still remain, while those on the left have all been demolished. These included Singer Sewing Machines, L&N, Walsh & Fielding Drapers, and McEwan boot and shoe warehouse. The Broad Street shopping centre opened here in 1988, with Bewleys as the anchor tenant upstairs.

John Roberts Square, c. 1963

This area of Broad Street and Barronstrand Street was pedestrianised in 2000, and renamed John Roberts Square in recognition of Roberts' contribution to Waterford architecture. Most of the cars seen here in the 1960s are either Ford Anglias or Prefects. In the centre are Coads shoe shop and Richard Gough's leather shop, while on the right, Woolworths, IMCO and Prescotts dry cleaners can be seen.

Barronstrand Street, Waterford

Barronstrand Street, *c.* 1900
The cathedral and its imposing railings are the focus of this picture. The railings were removed in the 1960s. To the right of the cathedral are the premises of Robert Cuttlar, stationery and hardware merchant – an unusual combination. The black street sign on the left-hand side says 'Glasgow House'. This was the original location for R. Coad, Boot and Show Warehouse. In the left foreground, farm machinery is displayed on the street outside the premises of William Power Ironmongery and Household Furniture.

The People's Park, Waterford. 915.

The People's Park, Bandstand, c. 1910

The park is situated on the old Lombard's marsh and was laid out in 1857. Mud from the quays and rubble from old houses in Barronstrand Street were used to fill in the marsh. Rock from a road realignment at Bilberry was used for the park wall. The park was formally opened by Lord Carlisle, the Lord Lieutenant, in August 1857. The bandstand was added in 1869.

The Park & Pleasure Grounds.   Waterford.
No. 12479

The Park Fountain, *c.* 1900

The fountain was added to the park in 1883, twenty-six years after the park first opened. It was a twin of the fountain in Bewley's Hotel in Ballsbridge, Dublin. The fountain was vandalised beyond repair in the 1980s and replaced by the present structure. Carlisle Bridge can be seen in the background. This bridge links the park to the courthouse.

Catholic Cathedral, Waterford.

Cathedral of the Most Holy Trinity, c. 1906

This cathedral was built in 1793 and is Ireland's oldest Catholic cathedral. The architect was John Roberts, who also designed Christ Church Cathedral twenty years earlier. The cost was £20,000. The original building was extended a number of times over the centuries. The sanctuary area was added in 1854, while the front façade of the cathedral was not completed until 1893. The railings in front were removed in the 1960s.

Interior of Cathedral of the Most Holy Trinity, c. 1906

The baldachin, or canopy over the altar, was erected in 1881. The distinctive carved oak baroque pulpit was installed in 1883, and is the work of Buisine and Sons of Lille, France. Initially, the ornate ceiling was in a Victorian polychrome style, but this was subsequently painted over. In 1977, following the Second Vatican Council, the altar area was refurbished and the new altar installed, facing the front. Ten chandeliers were gifted by Waterford Crystal in 1979. Major repairs to the building were also carried out in the 1990s and in 2006.

Christ Church Cathedral, *c.* 1908

A cathedral has stood on this site since 1096. It was here, in 1170, that Strongbow married Aoife and changed the course of Irish history, heralding in the Anglo Norman Age. The medieval cathedral was demolished in 1773 and the present cathedral was built. The architect was John Roberts, who went on to build the Catholic cathedral twenty years later. The spire was added in the 1880s. One of the pillars of the medieval cathedral has been exposed for viewing in the ante-chapel of the cathedral.

Interior of Christ Church Cathedral, c. 1880

The interior of Christ Church is pictured above, *c.* 1880. Extensive remodelling later took place during a Victorian restoration by Sir Thomas Drew between 1885 and 1891. The galleries were removed and the lower nave windows blocked up. The central stone and marble pulpit was removed to the side and reduced in height. The organ was also placed in the north side of the chancel. It is now back in its original position.

De La Salle College, c. 1915

The De La Salle Brothers first came to Waterford in 1887 and opened a primary school in Stephen Street. De La Salle College opened as a teacher training college at Newton in July 1894, for both members of the De La Salle order and other secular students. It remained as a training college until 1939, and in 1949, it became a secondary school. A number of extensions were added in 1974 and 2001. The statue of St John the Baptist was erected by past pupils around 1920 in memory of Brother Thomas, principal of the school between 1891 and 1912.

Presentation Convent, c. 1920

This building dates from 1842 and was designed by architect Augustus Pugin. It took a number of years to build, and it was 1848 before the Presentation nuns moved in. The chapel took another fifteen years to build and was not consecrated until 1863. The convent was sold in 2006, and, following extensive modernisation, reopened as Waterford Health Park in 2009.

Abbey Church Ferrybank, *c.* 1910

This church was built around 1820 by the Board of First Fruits. This was an institution of the Church of Ireland, established in 1711 to build and improve churches in Ireland. It was replaced by the Board of Ecclesiastical Commissioners in 1833. The Abbey church was used for Church of Ireland services up until the 1980s. It was then purchased by the Ferrybank Scouts and refurbished as their new den in 1990. The cemetery, which is now overgrown, contains the remains of many well-known Waterford merchants, including Henry Denny, founder of Denny's bacon empire.

The Tower Hotel, *c.* 1905

The block presently occupied by the Tower Hotel previously consisted of two blocks with Tower Lane in between. On the riverside was the Adelphi Hotel, built *c.* 1782. Next door was the headquarters of the Waterford Steam Ship Co. The second block consisted of a private residence and the Imperial Hotel. The Imperial Hotel was demolished in the early 1960s to make way for the Tower Hotel. The Adelphi Hotel was not demolished until 1970, and for a long time the space was used as a car park. It was not until 1989 that the Tower Hotel secured the site and lane between. The newly extended Tower Hotel opened in April 1991.

Irish Radium Products Ltd, *c.* 1940
This building started life as the city residence of the Congreve family of Mount Congreve, and was built in the early eighteenth century. It has had many other uses, including an orphanage, a boarding school, a printing works and a furniture store. At the time this photograph was taken it was a factory that made boot, shoe and floor polish. It later became the headquarters of IMCO Cleaners. It is now a bar and nightclub.

Woolworths, *c.* 1931

Woolworths opened in Waterford in November 1930, in the premises previously occupied by Walter Walsh & Sons. This store was similar to the present-day pound shops, as most of the items for sale were either 3*d* or 6*d*, as seen from the sign over the shop. The store closed in 1984, along with seventeen other Woolworths stores in the country. Both the Waterford and Wexford stores were sold to Primark, who opened Penneys stores.

Savoy Cinema, *c.* 1953

The Savoy Cinema opened in 1933, following the demolition of the premises of Power's Drapery. The opening night was a benefit night for Ballybricken church, and all proceeds were donated to its repair fund. In later years the cinema also functioned as a concert venue. The Savoy closed in June 1976. Supermacs fast food restaurant opened in the front lobby, while The Book Centre moved into the auditorium in August 1993.

Coady's Tobacconist, No. 33 The Mall, c. 1930

This famous building at No. 33 The Mall was built around 1835, as a townhouse for the Carews of Ballinamona. In 1848, it became the Wolfe Tone Confederate Club and it was here that Thomas Francis Meagher first unveiled the Tricolour in March 1848. Since then, it has had a number of occupants. At the end of the nineteenth century it was occupied by Whitehead Organ Builders. It then became Coady's Tobacconists. It operated as a tobacconist, sweet and confectionary shop over the next sixty years, with a number of different owners, and closed in the early 1960s. Further uses included an accountancy office, office for a waste disposal company, nightclub called The Leeson Club, and a restaurant. It is now Aoife's Café and Gallery.

Kelly's Garage, c. 1920

The first purpose-built garage in Ireland, it has retained much of its original character. William Peare opened the garage in 1900 in partnership with Sir William Goff. The premises had previously been a coach building works. It has remained a garage since then, albeit under different ownership, becoming Kelly's in 1917 and Barrett's in the 1990s.

Bishop Foy School, *c.* 1910
This school takes its name from its benefactor Bishop Nathaniel Foy (1648–1706). In his will, he left a substantial amount of money for the establishment of a school for the 'poor Protestants of Waterford'. Initially, it was situated in Barronstrand Street, but soon moved to Grantstown. In 1902, this purpose-built school was constructed on the Mall. It closed in June 1967, and was demolished soon afterwards. Waterford Crystal, formally the ESB offices, now stands on the site.

Bishop's Palace, *c.* 1930

At this time the Bishop's Palace was used as a boarding school for the Bishop Foy School. It operated as such from 1920 until the closure of the school in 1967. The building was then purchased by Waterford Corporation, and used as offices for their engineering department. In 2011, it was converted into the Bishop's Palace Museum. The palace was originally commissioned by Bishop Charles Este and built between 1741 and 1752.

Shaws, c. 1915

According to the National Inventory of Architectural Heritage, this building from 1840 is one of the earliest surviving purpose-built commercial ventures in the city. The firm Robertson, Ledlie, Ferguson & Co. was founded in 1853, and had premises in Waterford, Cork, Dublin and Belfast. Shaws purchased the Waterford store in 1941 and gradually expanded it by taking over the adjoining properties on the Quay. The sign of Robertson, Ledlie, Ferguson & Co. can still be seen on the Gladstone Street side of the building.

Downes, c. 1934

Established in 1797, the firm of Henry Downes began life as a spirit distribution business and has remained in the same family ever since. Today, it is one of the few remaining houses to bottle its own whiskey and now has ten separate blends. It was not until the 1960s that the pub part of the business developed. The building also includes a squash court.

Deevy's Drapery Shop, *c.* **1900**

Edward Deevy opened his drapery business in his hometown of Kilkenny. In 1876, he acquired this premises in Michael Street and relocated his drapery shop to Waterford. He died in 1896 and his son, also called Edward, took over the business. The men's clothing shop, Burtons, acquired the premises in 1928, demolished it and built an entirely new structure, which still stands today. Edward Deevy's daughter was the playwright Teresa Deevy.

Bridge Hotel, c. 1908

Built in 1895, this hotel is situated in one of the most prominent locations in the city, directly opposite the bridge. The gable fronted house on the left dates from c. 1820, and was demolished in 1970 when the hotel was extensively extended. It is now the new entrance to the hotel. The hotel has been known as the Bridge Hotel more or less since its construction. In the 1970s and early 1980s, a popular disco was held here; it was the favourite nightspot for most Waterford teenagers.

Clyde Shipping Office, *c.* 1910

The Clyde Shipping Co. was founded in 1820. In 1859, it launched the first service between Waterford and Glasgow. In 1912 it absorbed the Waterford Steamship Co. Two of its most famous ships were the Formby and the Coninbeg, which were both torpedoed by German U-Boats in December 1917. The SS *Rockabill* was the last of the Clyde steamers to operate from Waterford. The Clyde Shipping Office was originally built *c.* 1890. It was renovated around 1977 and the front entrance remodelled. An optician now occupies the ground floor.

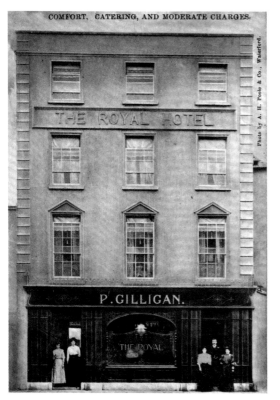

COMFORT, CATERING, AND MODERATE CHARGES.

THE ROYAL HOTEL

P. GILLIGAN.

Photo by A. H. Poole & Co., Waterford.

Royal Hotel, Lombard Street, *c.* **1910**
This hotel started life as the Milford Hotel, taking its name from the Mail Packet Steamer service, which left for Milford from Adelphi Quay nearby. It was extensively damaged by fire in 1908 and, following renovation, became the Royal Hotel. The proprietor was P. Gilligan, who also operated a grocery store on the ground floor. It operated as a hotel until the late 1940s and then continued as a licensed premises. In 1999, the Waterford soccer player Alfie Hale took it over as one of his sports bars. It operated as such for a number of years, until it was bought by the Tower Hotel. It remains empty today.

THE ROYAL BAR

Cummins Hotel, The Quay, c. 1880

This hotel is steeped in history. Originally owned by the Newport banking family, it was purchased by Thomas Meagher c. 1820. His son, Thomas Francis Meagher, was born here in 1823. Charles Bianconi then purchased the house and it became the Waterford terminus for his horse-drawn coaches. The building was demolished in the late nineteenth century and replaced by the Granville Hotel. Gradually, over the years, the Granville expanded; it now includes a number of adjoining buildings.

London and North Western Ticket Shop, *c.* 1910

The London and North Western Railway was one of the largest railway companies in the UK in the later part of the nineteenth century. They operated a steam packet service across the Irish Sea from Waterford. Their office was quite small and occupied one part of the adjoining Parade Hotel. The hotel was later sold and became Jordan's Bar. For a long time it was known as the American Bar due to the presence of the eagle on top of the building. The balconies still exist on the windows but are covered up by advertising banners.

Elysium House, Ballytruckle, *c.* 1891

Built originally as a family home *c.* 1820, Elysium House was purchased in 1824 by the Ursuline sisters, who had been in Waterford since 1816. New buildings were gradually erected in the grounds, including school buildings and a new convent. Elysium House returned to private hands around the turn of the twentieth century. Various families have lived there over the years, including Thomas Kelly, son of William Kelly, founder of Kelly's shop on the Quay. Today, a publishing business occupies the building.

Graves, *c.* 1900

The building supply firm of Graves was an institution in Waterford and New Ross for over 100 years. Founded in New Ross in 1811, it opened in Waterford in 1851. At the time these offices were built, in 1896, the premises extended over 4 acres and included an extensive steam-powered sawmill and private wharf. The business closed in 1985, and a service station and a number of commercial units now occupy the area.

The Park Shop, *c.* 1995

This shop was situated directly opposite the People's Park, and was a haven for children of all ages. For all the students of Waterpark College, De La Salle College and Newtown School, it was not only the shop for sweets, but also for cigarettes, which were sold individually. For younger children it was part and parcel of a visit to the park. It was run by the three Murphy sisters, who also had a love of the Irish language and would try to entice the shopper to a *cúpla focail*. The Murphy sisters also ran the Saint Philomena's Guest House next door. This building was previously the residence of John Horn, who was the master shipbuilder for the adjoining Neptune Yard in the mid-nineteenth century. Both the shop and guesthouse were demolished in 1997.

Plane Crash Barrack Street, 1920
During the War of Independence,
the IRA used mail interception as an
intelligence tactic. The British Army
then used planes for military
dispatches. On 17 November 1920,
one such plane hit a wireless aerial
as it flew over the infantry barracks,
lost control and crashed onto the roof
of the houses directly opposite the
barracks gate. Fortunately, no one was
seriously injured.

Manor Railway Station, c. 1950

Built in 1853, the Manor railway station was the Waterford terminus of the Tramore railway line. For generations of people, this railway station represented the start of a holiday in Tramore. Whether it was a day trip to the seaside, or a visit to the Tramore Races, the Tramore train represented excitement and fun. The line closed on 31 December 1960. The station was demolished in 1970. The terrace of houses in the bottom right, which were built c. 1880, are still standing today.

Lady Lane, c. 1986

This street is one of the oldest streets in the city and takes its name from Our Lady's chapel, which stood on the site of the present Franciscan church. The archway led into the premises of Paddy Hennessy, Undertaker, who also operated a transport business. This was formally the bottling store for T&H Doolans. The keystone at the top of the arch is inscribed 'T&HD 1906'. The adjoining Carnegie Library was originally built in 1903, and extended in 2003.

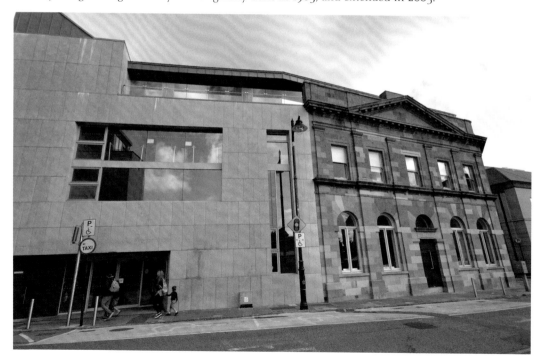

The Pier, Dunmore East, c. 1895

Until the early nineteenth century, shipping tended to bypass Dunmore East, berthing instead at Passage East or Cheekpoint. However, this changed in 1812, when Dunmore was chosen by the Post Office as the terminus for the mail packet route. The Scottish engineer Alexander Nimmo commenced work on building the pier in 1814, followed by the lighthouse in 1824.

Dunmore Harbour Co. Waterford.

Dunmore East Village, *c.* 1905

P. M. Egan wrote *History of Waterford* in 1894, around ten years before the view we see here. In it, he says about Dunmore East: 'We are now setting foot upon a prosperous, fashionable, aristocratic neighbourhood, which verily looks down upon all vulgar watering places along this southern coast. Tramore may be big and populous, Woodstown may be large and sublime, if empty, but let none of them dare to intrude when Dunmore, rich, retiring and genteel, comes to put itself in view.'

Dunmore East, Co. Waterford, Showing the Hotel, Post Office, and Coast Guard Station.

Dunmore East Village, *c.* 1910

Most of the buildings in this image date from the 1850s. On the right-hand side, Emerald Terrace remains virtually the same, although the house at the end has added a dormer window. This house has two plaques on its sidewall. One states that the international writer Patrick Lafcadio Hearn stayed there from time to time. The other plaque states that Patrick (Paddy Billy) Power, an award-winning coxswain of the Dunmore East Lifeboat, also lived there.

Market Square, Dungarvan

Valentine's Series

Market Square, Dungarvan, *c.* 1903

In the early nineteenth century, Dungarvan was replanned by the 5th and 6th Dukes of Devonshire. In his *History of Waterford*, published in 1894, Egan says of Dungarvan: 'Previous to 1815 the condition of this town was anything but beautiful or healthy. But since the re-edifying, which was carried out by the Duke of Devonshire, a complete change has taken place and Dungarvan now bids fair, soon, to rival any town of similar importance for its neatness and regularity.'

Market Square, Dungarvan

Market Square, Dungarvan, *c.* 1903

As part of the redevelopment of Dungarvan by the 5th and 6th Dukes of Devonshire, a new square and bridge, along with other streets, were also constructed. The square has been called Devonshire Square, Market Square and now Grattan Square. All the houses constructed in the square were three storey, except for two matching four-storey buildings built at the exit to Bridge Street. The wooden shed in the centre was a weigh house. This was replaced by a concrete building in the 1920s, and finally demolished in the 1960s.

THE SQUARE. DUNGARVAN CO. WATERFORD

Grattan Square, Dungarvan, c. 1951

By the 1950s, the donkeys and carts in Grattan Square had been replaced by motor cars. Most of the cars here are Volkswagen Beetles and Austin Devons. On close examination, their registration numbers can be seen. Most are KI, which was the original Waterford county registration, while WI was the city registration. The Bank of Ireland premises on the left dates from the 1940s. This building is now used by the Ulster Bank, while the Bank of Ireland has moved to the opposite side of the square.

Main Street, Dungarvan, *c.* 1911

Main Street, or Parnell Street, connected the new square built by the Duke of Devonshire to the old medieval town. The gable-ended building at the bottom of the street was the Old Market House. This was built in the late seventeenth or early eighteenth century on the site of the old town hall. Archaeological investigations date this town hall back to the middle of the seventeenth century. Today the building is used as an arts centre.

O'CONNELL STREET. DUNGARVAN. CO. WATERFORD

O'Connell Street, Dungarvan, *c.* 1950

This is another Dungarvan Street scene from the 1950s, when the donkey and cart had been replaced by the motor car. The car in front is a Ford Prefect with the registration plate KI 3489. The building at the corner on the right-hand side was previously the premises of Dunlea's model bakery, but had fallen into disrepair by the 1950s. This has now been replaced by a building with a canted entrance partly fronting to both streets.

Mary Street, Dungarvan, *c.* 1900

Looking east towards Grattan Square, the two distinctive four-storey buildings in the square (*mentioned earlier*) are still very identifiable. The Bank of Ireland building on the left has scaffolding up, and is obviously undergoing refurbishment. Mary Street was originally named William Street, after William Spencer Cavendish, the 6th Duke of Devonshire.

Davitt's Quay, Dungarvan, *c.* 1910

As part of the town improvements carried out by the Duke of Devonshire in the early 1800s, Davitt's Quay was also created. Unusually, here there are no ships berthed at the Quay. Other scenes from the time show the harbour thronged with schooners and fishing boats. In the background is the Devonshire Bridge, again financed by the Duke and completed in 1816. The bridge was built using rusticated sandstone imported from Cheshire and is still in use today.

QUAYS FROM ABBEYSIDE BRIDGE, DUNGARVAN.

Davitt's Quay, Dungarvan, c. 1910

Here is another view of the quay, this time looking south. The National Inventory of Architectural Heritage describes this quay as follows: 'Davitt's Quay is a structure of considerable significance in the locality, attesting to the various maritime activities that historically supported the economy of Dungarvan. The construction of the Quay in squared limestone blocks attests to high quality stone masonry. Now that much of the commercial maritime activity has ceased, the quay remains as an attractive and essential component of the townscape.'

Main Street, Lismore. Co. Waterford.

Main Street, Lismore, c. 1910

Although much of the town of Lismore dates from the nineteenth century, it was actually founded by Saint Carthage and his group of monks in AD 636. Today, Lismore has been designated one of the Heritage Towns of Ireland due to its unique character and beauty. It has won numerous awards in the Tidy Towns Competition, in addition to a gold award at the European Entente Florale Competition.

THE TOWN HALL, LISMORE

Town Hall, Lismore, *c.* 1950
The town hall was originally built *c.* 1815. It was renovated in 1890 when the clock tower was added. Damaged by fire during the War of Independence, it was again refurbished, and today serves as a heritage centre. The gable-fronted building on the corner, now the Red House Inn, was built sometime in the nineteenth century and served as an inn for coachmen.

H.M. THE KING LEAVING LISMORE CASTLE FOR A MOTOR DRIVE.

Lismore Castle, 1904

There has been a castle in Lismore since 1185, when King John built a *castellum* on the present site. It was used as a bishop's palace until the late sixteenth century. Sir Walter Raleigh owned it briefly before it was sold to Richard Boyle, First Earl of Cork. The present castle is mainly the work of the sixth Duke of Devonshire and dates from the mid-nineteenth century. In May 1904, King Edward VII visited Waterford and stayed as a guest of the Duke of Devonshire in Lismore Castle. The entrance door used by the King can be seen to the right of the courtyard below.

Lismore Hotel, *c.* 1955

The Lismore Hotel was built in 1797 by the Duke of Devonshire. As the castle had only twelve bedrooms, the hotel served as overflow accommodation for his guests. Known initially as the Lismore Inn, it was Ireland's first purpose-built hotel. On the wall outside there is a blue plaque dedicated to the writer William Thackeray, who stayed in the hotel when he visited Lismore in the 1840s.

View of Strand, Tramore

Tramore, c. 1915

Tramore began life as a small fishing village in the present Strand Street area. Its development as a seaside resort can be traced back to the mid-eighteenth century when the first lodging houses were built. Very soon, merchants from Waterford began to build large houses in the town and live there all year round. In 1863, 1,000 acres of the back strand were reclaimed from the sea by the Malcolmson family, and a racecourse and golf course were established there. However, a storm in 1911 breached the embankment completely, and both the racecourse and golf course had to move elsewhere.

95459 J.V.

...en's Bathing Place, Tramore

The Guillamene, *c.* **1915**
The Guillamene is well known to all visitors to Tramore. The natural depth of the water in this cove has been a magnet for swimmers for generations. The concrete steps were first erected by the Christian Brothers in the 1880s, and a diving board was erected in 1905. The sign at the top of the steps – 'men only' – is still there and reminds us of a different era.

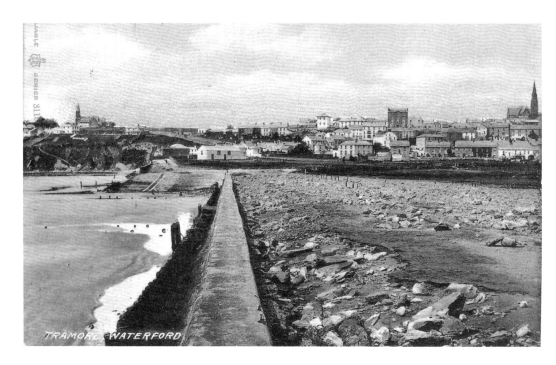

Tramore Promenade, c. 1905

Although it was in 1837 that the first sea wall was built at the western end of the strand, it was not until 1893 that this was extended towards the promenade area. The contractor was Richard Harney and it became known as Harney's Sea Wall. However, a violent storm three years later caused major damage. The current sea wall and promenade dates from 1913. Today the prom is a busy attraction and was the location for the Promenade Festival in July 2014, seen in the photograph below. The prom is now home to a monument to the crew of the Air Corps SAR helicopter, which crashed in the nearby sand dunes in dense fog in July 1999.

The Hydro, Tramore, c. 1955

Opened in 1948, The Hydro housed a number of sea baths. The staff included a physiotherapist, chiropodist and masseuse. A wide range of specialised physical treatment was available for rheumatic complaints and other conditions. The Hydro also had a restaurant. It was demolished in 1992, and is now the site for the amusement park. Amusement rides first visited Tramore in 1895. Tramore Fáilte was formed in 1963, and gradually the amusement park expanded.

Railway Station, Tramore, c. 1909

The Waterford Tramore railway line opened in 1853. The total distance travelled was 7.25 miles and the line took just seven months to build. It operated independently from 1853 until 1925, when it became part of the Great Southern Railways. It closed on 31 December 1960, and was replaced by a bus service. The Tramore train is remembered fondly by holidaymakers from all over the country. It was unique in that it was the only independent railway in the country that did not link with any other line.

Railway Square, Tramore.

Railway Square, Tramore, c. 1900
The ivy-covered building was the Marine Hotel, later the Deluxe Hotel and now the Sands Hotel. An unusual event took place in this square in 1947. On the night of 14 August, as the last train from Waterford approached the Tramore station, the brakes failed and the train ran straight out through the station wall in Railway Square, coming to a stop in front of the Sands Hotel. Luckily the couplings to the carriages had broken so they remained on the track, and no one was injured.

HOTEL MAJESTIC ★ ONE OF THE FINEST HOTELS ON THE IRISH COAST

TELEGRAMS : " MAJESTIC, TRAMORE "

TELEPHONES :
OFFICE 356
VISITORS 357

A.A., R.I.A.C. AND I.T.A. APPS.

THE HOTEL UNDOUBTEDLY OCCUPIES THE FINEST POSITION IN TRAMORE
STANDING IN ITS OWN GROUNDS WITH AN UNINTERRUPTED VIEW OF TRAMORE BAY.

Majestic Hotel, Tramore, c. 1940

The Majestic, originally known as Kelly's Hotel, was built in the early 1920s by John Kelly from Waterford. The same man purchased Peare's Motor Works in Catherine Street (the first garage in Waterford) and renamed it Kelly's Garage. In the 1940s it was taken over by the Breen family, who also owned the Bridge Hotel in Waterford. In 1977 it ceased trading as a hotel and was in the process of being converted into apartments when a fire broke out and the building was destroyed. In 1982, Tramore Fáilte purchased the ruins and redeveloped it as a hotel. Sold in 1987, it remains a hotel today.

Grand Hotel, Tramore, Co.Waterford.

The Grand Hotel, Tramore, c. 1910

The Grand Hotel opened as a hotel in 1795. It was first known as the Great Hotel. In 1824, the historian Richard Ryland says in his *History of Waterford*: 'The Great Hotel is a spacious building, elevated considerably above the village, and admirably adapted for enjoying the invigorating breezes from the sea.' Records show that, in 1915, the dress code for dinner was white tie and tails. The name was changed to the Grand Hotel in 1920. The hotel ceased trading in early 2014.

Bonmahon, c. 1950

In the mid-nineteenth century, Bonmahon became the centre of a thriving copper mining industry. About 2,000 people lived here in 1840. With twenty-one public houses in the village, drunkenness affected work in the mines, so the mine owners built a Temperance Hall. Other indications of the prosperity of the time were the existence of two hotels, a pawnshop, creamery, bacon factory and several shops. The mines closed in 1877 and the population declined. Today, there are just a few hundred people living in the village. Tom Hayes' pub on the left was built circa 1870, and the row of houses in the distance is Osborne Terrace, built c. 1830 for the use of miners.

Main Street, Ardmore, *c.* 1910

Ardmore is believed to be the oldest Christian settlement in Ireland. Saint Declan lived here in the late fourth century before the arrival of St Patrick in Ireland. The round tower in Ardmore dates from the twelfth century. Beside it are the ruins of an oratory from the eighth century and a thirteenth-century cathedral.

Ardmore, c. 1930

The Cliff House Hotel can be seen in the distance. Originally named Kelly's Hotel, it was built in the early 1900s. It underwent a major refurbishment in 2008 and is now the only five-star seaside hotel in the country. Today, Ardmore is a popular seaside resort with a long, sandy beach. It has won a number of awards in the Tidy Towns Competition and was the overall winner in 1992.

General View, Kilmacthomas

Kilmacthomas, *c.* 1938

One of the earliest references to Kilmacthomas in the history books is from the year 1649. In December of that year, Oliver Cromwell marched westwards, having failed to take the city of Waterford. However, when he reached Kilmacthomas, the River Mahon was flooded and he was unable to pass it. His army spent two nights in the field, which is now the public park. The bridge over the River Mahon dates from around 1800. The large building on the left is Stephenson's Woollen Mills, later Flahavans grain store. It has remained empty since 1999.

Portlaw, *c.* 1910

In 1825, David Malcolmson purchased a small flour mill on the River Clodagh and began building the largest cotton mill in the country. He then turned his attention to the nearby town of Portlaw, which he completely redesigned. It was laid out with a central square and six radiating streets. It was said that a policeman could stand in the square and observe every single street. Nearly 200 years later, Portlaw is still seen as one of the best examples of a planned industrial town.

Baile na nGall, An Rinn

Ballinagoul, *c.* 1910

The name *Baile na nGall* or *Ballinagoul* is translated from Irish as 'Homestead of the Foreigners'. Canon Power, in his *Place-Names of the Decies*, writes that 'a local tradition, which seems to be English in origin (and therefore unreliable), states that the foreigners were the crew of a Turkish vessel (Algerine Rover) which was wrecked here.' The small harbour was built by the Villiers Stuart family in 1828, and the pier was added in 1847. Although the famous Scottish engineer Alexander Nimmo drew up plans for a village, they were never proceeded with, and the village grew in a piecemeal fashion with a maze of laneways.

Ring College, *c.* 1955

Ring College was founded in 1906 in a small timber building beside the Helvic Road. In 1909, the college moved to the present building. This was originally intended as an industrial school, but was never completed. Mr Villiers Stuart of Dromana gave the premises to the Irish College Committee. A new wing was opened by Taoiseach Eamon de Valera in 1951. The college still operates today.

Cheek Point, Waterford.

Cheekpoint, *c.* 1930

Cheekpoint was a thriving village in the eighteenth century; it was the terminus for the mail packet service from London. The transfer of this service to Dunmore East in 1818 resulted in the residents of the village becoming dependent on fishing. The small fishing boats above are called prongs. The prong was a timber boat very similar to the widely known currach of the west coast. The design of the currach was simply copied for the river, where the boat could sit on the mud when the tide went out. Due to the tidal conditions, prongs were unique to Cheekpoint and other villages upriver.

Passage East on the River Suir, a busy fishing village.
The River Suir is noted for its salmon fishing.
Photo by A. H. Poole & Co,, 34 The Mall, Waterford.

Passage East, *c.* 1920
The village of Passage East takes its name from the Latin *passagium* or ferry. This ferry service across the estuary to County Wexford has existed here since ancient times. Being at the entrance to Waterford Harbour, in Norman times the village was put under the control of Waterford City, 7 miles away. It was not until 1842 that it became part of the Barony of Gaultier. The present car ferry has been operating since 1982.

Passage East, c. 1910
At this point in time, Passage East was a thriving fishing village. The census of 1911 shows that there were 134 households with a total population of 524. Of these, 100 were described as fishermen. Other occupations included merchant sailors and pilots. A fish house had been built in 1901 and could smoke fifty cran (about 38,000 fish) of herrings daily.

The Post Office & Hotel Saratoga, Woodstown, about 6 miles from Waterford.

Saratoga Pub, Woodstown, *c.* 1905

The Saratoga was originally built by a Capt. Coghlan in the mid-nineteenth century. It remained in family hands for many years. Originally a public house, the license was allowed to lapse for a long time during the early part of the twentieth century, but it remained a shop during that time. It is reputed that it was named after a returned emigrant from Saratoga in New York State. Backing on to Woodstown Strand, it is now a popular bar and restaurant.

Tallow, *c.* 1910

Although a settlement existed at Tallow since the thirteenth century, the medieval town was destroyed by fire in the late sixteenth century. The town was rebuilt in the early seventeenth century by Sir Richard Boyle, First Earl of Cork, as an English plantation. It was given a Royal Charter by James I in 1614. Most of the current buildings date from the nineteenth century, when the town underwent an economic expansion in industries including flour and brewing.

Main Street Cappoquin Co. Waterford.

Cappoquin, *c.* 1910

Cappoquin is another town built by Sir Richard Boyle. Indeed, his development of Cappoquin led the town to become the centre of an international arms trade in the seventeenth century. The Earl of Cork built his ironworks and cannon foundry here in the 1620s. The works specialised in cannon manufacture for the Thirty Years' War and were exported as far away as Amsterdam. Most of the current buildings date from the early to mid-nineteenth century. The church on the right is St Anne's church of Ireland, built *c.* 1800.

Cappoquin, c. 1900

There are two large bridges in the town. In the distance above, the railway bridge can be seen. This opened in 1878 as part of the Waterford–Dungarvan–Lismore line. Known as the Red Bridge, it is unusual in that the bridge is half stone and half iron; the metal section had higher arches for boat masts to pass through. Another view of this bridge can be seen on the following page. The road bridge in front was opened in 1851 and was built as a famine relief project.

The Steamship *Ness Queen*, Cappoquin, *c.* 1900

This steamship, owned and run by the Blackwater Navigation Service, came into service in 1897 and carried passengers from Youghal to Cappoquin – a distance of about 14 miles. She was a paddleboat and had a covered lounge and bar. This particular stretch of the Blackwater was known as the Irish Rhine due to the scenery and historic houses on its banks.

Aglish Village, *c.* 1910

The word Aglish comes from the Irish word *eaglais*, meaning 'church'. Canon Power, in his *Place Names of Decies*, states that it was also known as *Eaglais na nDéiseach*, or 'Aglish of the Decies', to distinguish from a second Aglish on the other side of the river. It is accepted that the church in question was an ancient parish church, which Power describes as 'pre-invasion'. Nearly all of the houses on the right-hand side are still standing and inhabited, although the thatched roofs have been replaced.

Stradbally Village — 19009.

Stradbally Village, *c.* 1900

Although Stradbally was founded in medieval times, most of the buildings in the square are from the early nineteenth century. Today, Stradbally is recognised as one of the prettiest villages in Ireland, achieving consistently high marks in the Tidy Towns Competition. In 1990 it won a bronze medal in the European Entente Florale, and subsequently won a gold medal in 2002.

Clashmore, *c.* 1900

Clashmore is one of the oldest villages in County Waterford. Saint Mochua founded the monastery and church of Clashmore in the seventh century. In the mid-nineteenth century, a distillery was built here by Lord Hastings and at its peak produced 20,000 gallons of whiskey annually. The building on the left was the old guards barracks, which stood on Chapel Lane.

Villierstown, *c.* 1900

The village of Villierstown was founded by the Villiers Stuart family in the 1740s. The intention was to develop a linen industry, and the village was initially populated with linen weavers from County Armagh. Initially the village had twenty-four houses, a schoolhouse, church, rectory, court house and police barracks. All of these buildings are still in the village today. The Irish name for Villierstown is Baile Nua, literally meaning 'new town'. Its most famous son is John Treacy, an athlete who won the World Cross Country Championships in 1979 and 1980, and won a silver medal in the marathon in the 1984 Olympics.

Picture Credits

National Roads Authority
p.5   Waterford City, 1373
       Drawn by Jonathan Millar and Sarah
       Nylund, Rubicon Heritage Services;
       reproduced by permission of the
       National Roads Authority.

Waterford Museum of Treasures
p.6   Waterford City, 1736

Waterford City Library
p.17   Ballybricken Fair, *c.* 1900
p.20   John Roberts Square, *c.* 1963
p.29   Presentation Convent, *c.* 1920
p.86   Saratoga Pub, Woodstown, *c.* 1905

Waterford City Archives,
Annie Brophy Collection
p.32   Irish Radium Products Ltd., *c.* 1940
p.33   Woolworths, *c.* 1931
p.34   Savoy Cinema, *c.* 1953
p.35   Coady's Tobacconist, No. 33 The Mall,
       c. 1930

National Library of Ireland
p.36   Kelly's Garage, *c.* 1920
p.37   Bishop Foy School, *c.* 1910
p.38   Bishop's Palace, *c.* 1930
p.39   Shaws, *c.* 1915
p.40   Downes, *c.* 1934
p.41   Deevy's Drapery Shop, *c.* 1900
p.42   Bridge Hotel, *c.* 1908
p.43   Clyde Shipping Office, *c.* 1910
p.45   Cummins Hotel, The Quay, *c.* 1880
p.46   London and North Western Ticket
       Shop, *c.* 1910
p.48   Graves, *c.* 1900
p.50   Plane Crash Barrack Street, 1920
p.84   Passage East, *c.* 1920

Waterford County Museum
p.44   Royal Hotel, Lombard Street, *c.* 1910
p.47   Elysium House, Ballytruckle, *c.* 1891
p.51   Manor Railway Station, *c.* 1950
p.55   Dunmore East Village, *c.* 1910
p.80   Kilmacthomas, *c.* 1930
p.81   Portlaw, *c.* 1910
p.88   Cappoquin, *c.* 1910
p.91   Aglish Village, *c.* 1910
p.92   Stradbally Village, *c.* 1900
p.93   Clashmore, *c.* 1900
p.94   Villierstown, *c.* 1900

Library of Congress
Front Cover: Reginald's Tower, *c.* 1895
Back Cover: Waterford City, *c.* 1895
p.6   Waterford City, *c.* 1895
p.8   City from Cromwell's Rock, *c.* 1895
p.10   Reginald's Tower, *c.* 1895
p.13   Parade Quay, *c.* 1895
p.53   The Pier, Dunmore East, *c.* 1895
p.89   Cappoquin, *c.* 1900

Paul O'Farrell
p.31   The Tower Hotel, *c.* 1905
p.87   Tallow, *c.* 1910

Oliver Lupton
p.49   The Park Shop, *c.* 1995

Pat Hennessy
p.52   Lady Lane, *c.* 1986

Mick Malone (Deise Aerial Photography)
p.5   Waterford City, 2014

Declan McGrath
p.31   The Tower Hotel, 2010

Cork Harbour Through Time

Kieran McCarthy and Daniel Breen

This fascinating selection of photographs traces some of the many ways in which Cork Harbour has changed and developed over the last century.

978 1 4456 3419 7

96 pages, full colour

Available from all good bookshops or order direct from our website www.amberleybooks.com